Cassandra

AN ESSAY BY

Florence
Nightingale

Introduction by MYRA STARK
Epilogue by CYNTHIA MACDONALD

THE FEMINIST PRESS
AT THE CITY UNIVERSITY OF NEW YORK
NEW YORK CITY

With grateful acknowledgment to Carolyn G. Heilbrun for her kind assistance.

**Library of Congress
Cataloging in Publication Data**
Nightingale, Florence, 1820–1910.
   Cassandra : an essay.
   Includes bibliographical references.
   1. Women—England—Social conditions—19th century. 2. Women—England—History—19th century.
3. Women—Psychology. 4. Upper classes—England—History. I. Title.
HQ1599.E5N54 1979
301.41' 2' 0942
79-15175 ISBN 0-912670-55-X

Grateful acknowledgment is made for permission to reprint the following copyrighted material: Cynthia Macdonald, "Florence Nightingale's Parts." Copyright © 1979 by Cynthia Macdonald. Reprinted by permission of the author. From the forthcoming book W(HOLES), to be published by Alfred A. Knopf.

The Feminist Press gratefully acknowledges the assistance of the Yale Medical Library in New Haven, Connecticut.

Cover and text design by Susan Trowbridge

Table of Contents

Introduction

By Myra Stark

"WHO IS MRS. NIGHTINGALE?" asked the London newspaper article which first brought her to public attention in October 1854; and the answer it gave fixed Florence Nightingale in the popular imagination of her time as a "ministering angel," the haloed lady with the lamp, soothing the fevered brows of wounded soldiers in the hospitals of the Crimea.[1] All England sang songs about "The Shadow on the Pillow" and "The Soldier's Cheer." She was worshiped as the ideal image of the tender, nurturing female—an image which still clings to her, as well as to the profession which she created.

The reality, however, was rather different. Even during the few years when she actually nursed, the legend was only part of the truth. Nursing, she wrote to Sidney Herbert at the War Office, was the least important of the functions she performed in the hospitals of Scutari and Balaclava.[2] Her accomplishments during the disastrous years the British Army experienced in the Crimea were more the result of her concern with diet and dirt and drains, her understanding of sanitation and its relation to mortality, her ability to organize, to lead, to get things done.

Although Florence Nightingale has remained enshrined in the popular imagination as the prototype of the saintly nurse, her few years of nursing were merely prelude: "her real life began," said Lytton Strachey in *Eminent Victorians*, "when, in the popular imagination, it had ended."[3] "I can never forget,"[4] she wrote over and over again in private notes after she was back in England—referring to the horror of the Crimea, which, she saw clearly, was the result of the incompetence and criminal negligence of the Army Medical Corps and of the War Office itself. She became the leader of a reform movement, the force behind the government commissions—giving evidence, drafting ordinances, writing reports. One cause led her inevitably to another—from reform of the Army Medical Services and the War Office to concern over hospital construction, sanitation, the living conditions of the British Army in India, hospitals in India, Indian sanitation and irrigation. She never visited India, but so great was her knowledge of Indian sanitary and army affairs that no important government official left for that country without seeing her; she directed the purification of the Madras water system from her bedroom in South Street, London.

In 1860, using funds sent to her by the general public, she founded the Nightingale School and Home for Nurses at St. Thomas' Hospital in London, and the following year, she created the Training School for Midwives at the King's College Hospital. In establishing these institutions, she was creating a new profession for women that was respectable and well paid at a time when women had few ways of earning a decent livelihood. She founded district nursing and workhouse nursing; she brought the field of public health to national attention. She was one of the first in Europe to grasp the principles of the new science of statistics and to apply them to military and civilian hospitals. As late as 1947, the Select Committee on Estimates, reporting on a cost-accounting system for the Army Medical Services, noted with surprise how well it worked: Florence Nightingale had devised it in 1861.[5] Although Nightingale never held public office nor any public position after her return from the

Crimea, her back bedroom in South Street was referred to as the "little War Office," and in it she did "more work," one biographer comments drily, "than most cabinet ministers."[6] She refused Queen Victoria's offer of an apartment in Kensington Palace because it was not close enough to the public officials with whom she worked daily. Even when she was well into her eighties, most official papers on Army sanitation and medical affairs were routinely sent to her for criticism; indeed, when the War Office misplaced a document, they often sent over to Florence Nightingale for her copy. When she moved, her statistical reports on Indian Army Stations alone required several vans to transport.

Each of Nightingale's interests would have been sufficient to occupy the working life of one conscientious individual; her life encompassed them all. In 1907, three years before her death, Florence Nightingale received the Order of Merit from King Edward VII—the first woman to be so honored. It was an appropriate tribute to a life of spectacular achievement.

IN AN AGE which believed that the essence of femininity was to live for others, Florence Nightingale was revered for her sacrifices for the sick and wounded; the real self-sacrifice for her, however, would have been to stay home, marry, and lead the life of a wealthy woman.

Born in 1820, Florence Nightingale was the daughter of William Edward Nightingale, a cultured, well-to-do Englishman who taught his daughters Greek and Latin, philosophy, and modern languages, and Fanny Smith Nightingale, a woman who enjoyed the pleasures of fashionable society. The Nightingales led the life of wealthy, upper-class English people during the nineteenth century—an existence of ease and leisure. Their two children, Florence and Parthenope, were named after the European cities in which they were born during a two-year wedding trip. The family spent the summers at Lea Hurst, their estate in Derbyshire, and the winters at Embley Park in Hampshire; there were visits to London for the spring and autumn seasons and long trips abroad, lasting a year or eighteen months at a time. The family on both sides was large—Florence Nightingale had twenty-seven first cousins —and long visits, frequent letters, and lavish parties were the rule: eighty people were housed at the Nightingales' for one Christmas party.

As a girl and young woman, Nightingale conformed outwardly to what was expected of her. She was attractive, well read, and witty; she had a great zest for life, loved to travel, and enjoyed parties and social life. But the existence that her parents and her world expected her to lead she saw ultimately as empty and wearisome.

VICTORIAN ENGLAND was a country in the grip of an ideology that worshiped the woman in the home. Women were viewed as wives and mothers, as potential wives and mothers, or as failed wives and mothers. The woman who was neither wife nor mother was called "the odd woman" or "the redundant woman."

Woman was the center of the age's cult of the family, "the angel in the house," tending the domestic altar. She was viewed as man's inferior—less rational, weaker, needing his protection; but, at the same time, she was exalted for her spirituality, her moral influence. Man was the active one, the doer; woman was the inspirer and the nurturer. The spheres of work in the world and in the home were rigidly divided between the sexes.

The laws of England were the bulwark of this ideology. Husbands had total economic power over their wives. Unless protected by private agreements, a wife's assets—her money, her property, even her children and her own body —were legally her husband's to dispose of. Thus the law completed what social and cultural tradition prescribed.

The vast majority of women in mid-Victorian England could not afford to live according to the feminine ideal of the period. While any destiny other than that of wife and mother was "unthinkable" for women of Nightingale's circle, many middle-class women did in fact remain single. They were often forced to earn their living as governesses—a poorly paid and sometimes humiliating position akin to that of a servant—or as dressmakers or milliners. The universities and professional employment were, of course, closed to women. Poor women were employed in factories, especially in textile mills, where they worked under the most inhumane conditions for twelve or fourteen hours a day.[7] Usually their wages were half those earned by men—not enough for subsistence.[8] Many supplemented these meager wages by working as prostitutes.

The majority of working women in Nightingale's day were domestics; they formed part of the growing army of household servants—cooks, housemaids, nannies, charwomen—demanded by the families of the new industrial magnates as well as by those of the aristocracy. Basically, there were two classes of women—one who in theory, if not in practice, was freed from any kind of labor, and the other who performed every form of household drudgery and menial work. The perfect lady was encouraged to leave work to her less fortunate sisters, to be "disfunctional and idle,"[9] an ornament to her family. As such she embodied the feminine ideal of the age—a combination of "sexual innocence, conspicuous consumption, and the worship of the family hearth."[10]

A flood of books and magazines promulgated this ideal. Among the most popular of the era were Mrs. Ellis's series, *The Daughters of England, The Wives of England, The Mothers of England;* Mrs. Beeton's *Book of Household Management; The British Mother's Magazine;* and *The Ladies' Companion at Home and Abroad.* Middle- and upper-class women were to devote themselves to getting married and to being a credit to their husbands; whatever education they received had this end in view. They were to command their servants, to oversee the education and moral training of their children, to grace their husband's table, to dress to please. They were encouraged to do needlework and "fancy work"; to dabble in drawing, painting, and music; to read and write letters; and to visit. The sphere of the lady was extended to include cultural events and such charitable work as visiting the sick and carrying soup and clothing to the poor—activities that were seen as extensions of innately female qualities of nurturing.

IT WAS A LIFE Florence Nightingale grew to loathe. In her many letters and in her private notes, she poured out her detestation of the life of the idle woman, made up, as her friend Mary Clarke wrote, of "faddling, twaddling and the endless tweedling of nosegays in jugs."[11] In 1846, Nightingale wrote:

What is my business in this world and what have I done this fortnight? I have read the 'Daughter at Home' to Father and two chapters of Mackintosh; a volume of Sybil to Mamma. Learnt seven tunes by heart. Written various letters. Ridden with Papa. Paid eight visits. Done company. And that is all.[12]

Her mother put her in charge of the still-room, the pantry, and the linen-room, sent her abroad whenever Florence's discontent seemed particularly severe, and could not understand why she was not satisfied with parties and visits and reading and embroidery—above all, why she would not marry. Any deviation from the prescribed pattern aroused her mother's opposition: when Florence wanted to learn mathematics instead of doing needlework, Mrs. Nightingale forbade it as unsuitable; only the intervention of a favorite aunt won for Florence two lessons a week, chaperoned, with a clergyman.

"The position of a single woman of thirty in the middle classes," said a contemporary of Florence Nightingale's in 1868,

is horrible. Her cares are to be properly dressed, to drive or walk or pay calls with Mamma; to work miracles of embroidery—but for what? What we want is something to do, something to live for.[13]

That, of course, is exactly what Florence Nightingale wanted: "I craved for some regular occupation," she wrote, "for something worth doing instead of frittering my time away on useless trifles."[14] Such longings fill her private notes in the forties and fifties: "A profession, a trade, a necessary occupation, something to fill and employ all my faculties, I have always felt essential to me, I have always longed for, consciously or not."[15]

Most significant in her rebellion against the conventional life of women is that she saw it as a waste of time and abilities. She was an energetic, intelligent woman who wanted to put her capabilities to use. "Such a *head*," Queen Victoria marveled after talking to Florence Nightingale. "I wish we had her at the War Office."[16] The discrepancy between what she was capable of doing and what she was permitted to do in her young womanhood was torture for her.

During these early years, Nightingale's friendships with women—Mary Clarke, Marianne Nicholson, and Hilary Bonham Carter—provided her with outlets for her rebellious feelings and served as sources of strength. Mary Clarke (the "Clarkey" of Nightingale's letters), an Englishwoman who had escaped to Paris from the restrictive life of Victorian England and become an influential literary and political figure, strengthened Nightingale's determination to choose a better way of life for herself, by helping her to articulate her criticism of the life she was expected to lead. "Why," Clarkey asked, "don't they [women] talk about interesting things? Why don't they use their brains?"[17]

Nightingale's friendship with Lord Ashley, the reformer, also provided her restless discontent with a direction. After she met him, she began to focus her energies on the subject matter that would preoccupy her for the rest of her life. She got up long before the family every morning and filled vast numbers of notebooks with detailed information drawn from blue books and reports on medical and sanitary conditions in hospitals all over Europe. Then the bell for breakfast rang, and she was obliged to come down to dawdle over the meal and sit idle in the library while her father read aloud from the newspaper.

As the years passed, she spent more and more time in daydreaming, escaping in fantasy from the restrictions of her life. She was terrified of this habit of hers; she considered it either a symptom of mental illness or a sin. "I see," she wrote, "so many of my kind who have gone mad for want of something to do."[18] And she recorded in great detail her struggles against this habit. Of the specific forms her daydreams assumed, she was silent, but she indicated clearly that they were dreams of heroic action. She also recorded how she fell into "trance-like" states as an escape from the boredom and tedium of social life—at dinner parties, for example. "Why, Oh my God cannot I be satisfied with the life that satisfies so many people?" she wrote. "What am I that their life [the life of her family] is not good enough for me? . . . The thoughts and feelings that I have now I can remember since I was six years old. . . .[19] I am told that the conversation of all these good clever men ought to be enough for me. Why am I starving, desperate, diseased on it?"[20] In the daydreams she projected her ideal of an heroic life of action; once she found her work in the world, all mention of the daydreams vanishes from her private papers.

religion = service

AN ESSENTIAL ELEMENT in finding her work in the world was her intensely religious nature. Like that of so many Victorians, hers was a religion of service; she believed that one serves God best by doing good work in this world. In a private note, she wrote, "On February 7th, 1837, God spoke to me and called me to His service."[21] Almost forty years later, in another private note, she recorded four such calls at key points in her lifetime.[22] It is clear that these moments of inner conviction were for her the manifestation of God's will, making plain where her work lay. Throughout her life, autobiographical notes indicate ceaseless soul-searching, constant examination of her life to see if she was doing enough and accomplishing enough.

After her initial "call," five years passed while she struggled to see where and how she could serve. During that time she came to believe that marriage, at any rate, would make a life of heroic service impossible. Her private notes and letters testify to this growing realization: "Women don't consider themselves as human beings at all," she wrote. "There is absolutely no God, no country, no duty to them at all, except family. . . ."[23] "Ladies' work," she said, "has always to be fitted in; where a man is, his business is the law."[24] The only man whom she loved was Richard Monckton Milnes, the intellectual and social reformer. She refused to marry him, however, and it was for her an agonizing refusal. "I have an intellectual nature which requires satisfaction," she wrote,

and that would find it in him. I have a passionate nature which requires satisfaction and that would find it in him. I have a moral, an active, nature which requires satisfaction and that would not find it in his life. Sometimes I think I will satisfy my passional nature at all events, because that will at least secure me from the evils of dreaming. But would it? I could be satisfied to spend a life with him in combining our different powers in some great object. I could not satisfy this nature by spending a life with him in making society and arranging domestic things.[25]

9

She viewed marriage as an extension of her life with her family, and "I know I could not bear his life," she said: "to be nailed to a continuation, an exaggeration of my present life without hope of another would be intolerable to me . . . voluntarily to put it out of my power ever to be able to seize the chance of forming for myself a true and rich life would seem to me like suicide."[26] Years later, when her highly trained "Nightingale nurses" married, she viewed each marriage as a desertion. In an autobiographical note on the subject of marriage, she wrote, "I must strive after a better life for women,"[27] and in another note, exclaimed, "Oh God, no more love. No more marriage, O God."[28]

Finally, however, Nightingale saw clearly what form her service was to take. The one activity besides social and cultural ones Victorian women were encouraged to pursue outside the home was philanthropic charity, visits to the poor and the sick. Such activity was considered a legitimate extension of women's innate capacities for nurturing. It is not at all surprising that many well-to-do Victorian women who, like Florence Nightingale, were restless for serious occupation, should have turned to charity: it was considered ladylike and it had social approval. But Nightingale spoke contemptuously of women who dabbled in "poor peopling," and saw the defects in a system which left the care of the sick to untrained women following, often sporadically, benevolent impulses. If it was work that needed to be done, it should be done seriously. She wanted training and knowledge. That desire was the beginning of a long and bitter conflict with her family. Not only did she want to work—a pursuit considered unladylike except in cases of dire necessity, and then regarded with pity—but she wanted to nurse—an occupation considered unthinkable. "It was as if I had said I wanted to be a kitchen-maid," she wrote.[29]

In the 1840s, with the exception of the Catholic nursing orders and the very few Protestant nursing orders, nursing as a profession did not exist. It was a poorly paid job. Most nurses were untrained women, drawn from the poor. Naturally, the well-to-do sick stayed at home and were nursed by the women of their own family, since all women were thought to have an innate capacity to nurse.

It took Florence Nightingale nine years of conflict with her family before she succeeded in leaving home, at the age of thirty-two, for training at the Institution for Deaconesses at Kaiserwerth on the Rhine. On her return from Kaiserwerth, in 1853, she accepted her first post, as Superintendent of an Establishment for Gentlewomen during Illness on Harley Street, in London. In the same year, her father made her financially independent, settling on her £500 a year. One year later came the Crimea—and her work began.

"CASSANDRA" WAS WRITTEN in 1852, at a time in Florence Nightingale's life when she despaired: "My present life is suicide," she wrote. "My God what will become of me?"[30] "Cassandra" emerged out of the long years of almost immobilizing desperation, out of the bitterness of thwarted desires, and the writing of it seemed to free her. It was as if she hardened her resolve to escape by relentlessly analyzing what it was she had to escape from. She discovered after the writing of "Cassandra," as her biographer Cecil Woodham-Smith notes, that the bonds which confined her were made of straw, and that it was possible to break them. Through the writing of "Cassandra," despair was transformed into rebellion.[31] In 1852 she wrote to her father, "I hope now I have come into possession of myself";[32] and, in an imaginary conversation with her mother at the same time, she wrote, "I shall go out and look for work to be sure. . . . You must now consider me married or a son."[33]

Reflecting the years and the conditions which produced it, "Cassandra" is a work of despair and anger. The essay begins with a cry of anguish for "suffering, sad, 'female humanity!' ''It goes·on to present the life of the middle- and upper-class Victorian woman as a chronicle of waste and frustration, as a death in life.

The most radical criticism ''Cassandra'' levels at the lives of women is directed at their status as contingent beings who must fit their lives to the needs of others. Women, says Florence Nightingale, ''never have an half-hour in all their lives . . . that they can call their own, without fear of offending or hurting someone else.'' Such a life must exclude any serious work or study, since the demands of either would make a woman unavailable to others. ''So women play through life!''—taking up and putting down one activity after another. The sight of a room full of men doing needlework or a carriage of men driving out for an afternoon's ride would be laughable, Nightingale points out, because a man's time is valuable; a woman's time, however, is defined as a thing of no value, which must be filled up.

Denied work or training, their time invaded, women are condemned to living through others and for others, first as daughters, subordinate to the family, then as wives, reflexes of their husbands. Although young women regard marriage as their only chance to escape from the boredom and suffocation of their lives within the family, most find that they have succeeded merely in exchanging one form of tyranny for another. Nightingale's analysis of marriage is unsparing. A woman must ''annihilate'' herself in the life of her husband; she must ''dedicate herself to the vocation of her husband.'' As a result, however inadequate it may be, the marriage becomes, of necessity, a woman's whole life. ''Women think about marriage much more than men do,'' writes Nightingale. ''It is the only event of their lives.'' She saw that most men do not see real women, but rather images they themselves have called into being, and that marriage is severely limited by myths about women's nature. She also saw very clearly the economic implications of denying women any other means of support except through husband or father.

"The woman who has sold herself for an establishment," Nightingale asks, "in what way is she superior to those we may not name?"

These unnatural restrictions and denials are the cause of the anguish that marks the lives of women. Thwarted energy and suppressed unhappiness lead to incessant daydreaming, the narcotic addiction of women. Prophetically anticipating a twentieth-century analysis of women's psychology, Florence Nightingale sees that most women do not rebel against the conditions of their lives, but rather escape into their inner lives, to fantasy, depression, or illness:

What these women suffer—even physically—from the want of such work no one can tell. The accumulation of nervous energy, which has nothing to do during the day, makes them feel every night, when they go to bed, as if they were going mad.

"Cassandra," then, is an outcry of protest against the powerlessness of women—their lack of control over their lives, their subordination to husband and family, their loss of any identity except through personal relationships—and against the boredom and triviality that result from the limitations of their existence. It is also a statement of protest against the waste of women's energies and talents, a statement that Virginia Woolf was to echo in her elegy for Shakespeare's hypothetical sister in *A Room of One's Own,* an essay which acknowledges "Cassandra."[34]

At the end of "Cassandra," Florence Nightingale turns to the future, and calls on women to "Awake, . . . all ye that sleep, awake." "The time is come," she says, "when women must do something more than tend the 'domestic hearth'." Recognizing how poor is the position of women in the nineteenth century, indeed how much it has deteriorated since the previous century, she looks to the next century for a leader to emerge. Christ's great contribution to the advancement of women, she notes, was to raise them above slaves, "mere ministers to the passion of man," and to endow them with a moral life and an independent relation to God. "The next Christ," she suggests, "will perhaps be a female Christ." Thus, it is not surprising that Nightingale included "Cassandra" in a volume of her religious writings, privately printed in 1860. There is some evidence among her papers that she had originally planned to write a novel and that "Cassandra" is what remained of that plan.[35] But she considered it a religious work, a statement against the waste of souls, against lives lived without any meaning or purpose, and she put it in volume two of *Suggestions for Thought,* a volume of "Practical Deduction," containing criticism of the religious and social life of her day.

In "Cassandra," Florence Nightingale wrote movingly and sensitively of the plight of Victorian women of her social class. Considered as a political work, "Cassandra" should rightly take its place among the classics of Victorian feminism. It belongs with such works as John Stuart Mill's *The Subjection of Women* (1869), Barbara Leigh Smith Bodichon's *A Brief Summary in Plain Language of the Most Important Laws Concerning Women* (1854), Bessie Rayner Parkes' *Essays on Women's Work* (1865), Josephine Butler's *Women's Work and Women's Culture* (1869), Emily Davies' *The Higher Education of Women* (1866), Mrs. Hugo Reid's *A Plea for Women* (1843), Jessie Boucherett and Helen Blackburn's *The Condition of Working Women and the Factory Acts* (1896)—all nineteenth-century works in which assumptions about the lives and roles of women are examined and criticized.

Florence Nightingale was not alone in her criticism of the idle and useless lives to which middle-class women were routinely consigned. She is to be seen in context with that band of women in England in the last half of the nineteenth century who struggled to establish women's right and need to enter the world of education and work: Barbara Leigh

Smith Bodichon, Bessie Rayner Parkes, Josephine Butler, Jessie Boucherett, Millicent Garrett Fawcett, Emily Davies, Dorothea Beale, Frances Buss, Jemima Clough, Sophia Jex-Blake, Frances Power Cobbe, Elizabeth Garret Anderson, and Emily Faithfull, among many others. Florence Nightingale's work in the Crimea began in 1854. In 1858, *The Englishwoman's Journal* began printing, superseded in 1866 by *The Englishwoman's Review of Social and Industrial Questions,* which published monthly until 1910. These magazines were the voice of the Ladies of Langham Place, a group of feminists determined to improve the condition of women. In 1857, they set up the Society for Promoting the Employment of Women. When vast numbers of desperate women begged the Society for help, the Langham Place feminists realized how severe and widespread was the need for education, training, and employment opportunities for women. They began the long struggle to open the universities to women, to get women into medical schools and certified as doctors, to enlarge and extend the fields of work women could enter. Emily Faithful set up The Victoria Press to print the magazines; it was the first press to employ women. Year after year, the papers read at the National Society for the Promotion of the Social Sciences, the forum for the most progressive social ideas in England and supportive of women from its inception in 1854, document women's struggles to acquire training and work.

In spite of the obvious affinity between Nightingale's ideas, as put forth in "Cassandra," and the goals of the women's movement of her time, one cannot exactly say that Nightingale was, in modern terms, a feminist. She refused to give wholehearted support to the main feminist causes of her day—suffrage and equal educational rights for women—and was critical of those who did. Indeed, she frequently expressed contempt for the lives and characters of most women. In a letter to her friend Clarkey, for example, she wrote:

Women crave *for being loved,* not for loving. They scream at you for sympathy all day long. They are incapable of giving *any* in return, for they cannot remember your affairs long enough to do so. . . . They cannot state a fact accurately enough to another, nor can that other attend to it accurately enough for it to become information.[36]

"I am," she wrote to Harriet Martineau, "brutally indifferent to the rights and wrongs of my sex. And I should have been equally so to any controversy as to whether woman ought or ought not to do what I have done for the Army."[37] In a later work, *Notes on Nursing,* Nightingale concludes with an attack on the "jargon about the rights of women," urging women not to do all that men do simply because men do it. The death of Agnes Jones, a Nightingale matron, head of the Liverpool Infirmary, brought a bitter note about the "enormous jaw, the infinite female ink . . . on 'Woman's Work'."[38] "It makes me mad," Nightingale said, "the 'Women's Rights' talk about the 'want of a field for them'. . . ."[39]

How does one account for the apparent contradiction between these later remarks and her impassioned plea on behalf of women in "Cassandra"? In part, some of her expressions of contempt for women's superficiality and self-indulgence can be seen as a bitter response to her early years of suffocation at the hands of her mother and sister, who tried to force her to conform to the feminine ideals of the day, and with whom she had endured years of bitter conflict before she was able to leave home and go to work. Only her fame after the Crimea changed their attitude toward her, she commented bitterly. When she tried to work in London, they descended upon her and made her work impossible. She wrote to her friend Clarkey:

The whole occupation of Parthe and Mama was to lie on two sofas and tell one another not to get tired by putting flowers into water. . . . It is a scene worthy of Molière, where two people in tolerable and even perfect health lie on the sofa all day and persuade themselves and others that they are the victims of their self-devotion for another who is dying of overwork.[40]

Shortly after her return from the Crimea, Florence Nightingale became an invalid, expected by her doctors to die at any time; she remained bedridden until she was well into her sixties, though she produced over two hundred books, pamphlets, and reports, and over twelve thousand letters, most related in one way or another to her work. Sir George Pickering, in *Creative Malady,* sees her illness as "a psychoneurosis with a purpose," a "protective" illness that freed her from the presence of her family and, while isolating her as an invalid in her room, permitted her to do her work.[41] Pickering argues for the hysterical nature of her "heart weakness," the attacks which threatened each time her mother or sister approached. After Mrs. Nightingale transferred her center of interest to Florence's sister Parthe upon the latter's marriage, the situation eased. Pickering also points out that it was only after Mrs. Nightingale's death that Florence Nightingale, then in her sixties, left her bed and reentered the world. It appears, then, that much of Florence Nightingale's criticism of women was evoked by the examples of her mother and sister, and originated in her difficult relationship with them.

Once she had, more or less, freed herself from the suffocating circumstances of her family upbringing, Nightingale focused almost exclusively on her work. "I am," she wrote revealingly in a letter late in life, "soaked in work."[42] This exclusive concentration of hers on work is a major reason for her impatience with women, most of whom could not work as she did. Indeed, the emphasis on work led Nightingale to identify with men. She refers to herself over and over again as a "man of action," or a "man of business." Men were free to follow her and to work with her; she held it against women that they were not. Having escaped from the life of enforced idleness which she described with such compassion in "Cassandra," she began to overlook the fourteen years of struggle which had preceded that escape. Like so many women of achievement, she felt that if she had succeeded in surmounting the repressive circumstances of her youth, other women could, too. Their failure to do so she saw as a failure of will.

Because of her active and practical nature she was impatient with women who talked about educational equality—this "enormous jaw, the infinite female ink"—instead of buckling down to the world's work. Her condemnation of those who complained of women's exclusion from medical school was based on her awareness of the desperate need for capable women to train as nurses. "We can't find the women," she complained. "They won't come." If she was angered by "the 'Women's Rights' talk about the 'want of a field for them' . . . ," it was evidently because she had already found a field for them and could not understand why they did not rush to fill it. It is in this context that many of her apparently antifeminist remarks must be understood.

Similarly, her attitude toward women's suffrage must be examined in light of her attitude toward work. When John Stuart Mill asked her, in 1867, to join the National Society for Women's Suffrage, she refused; her explanation, however, indicates that her refusal was based not on political disagreement but rather on her belief that women's economic struggle was more important than suffrage and in danger of being undermined by the exclusive concentration on it: "That women should have the suffrage," she wrote to Mill,

I think no one can be more deeply convinced than I. It is so important for a woman to be a "person," as you say. . . . But it will be years before you obtain the suffrage for women. And in the meantime there are evils which press much more hardly on women than the want of suffrage. . . . my experience tells me that women, and especially poor and married women, are most hardly pressed upon now. . . . Till a married woman can be in possession of her own property, there can be no love or justice. . . . Is it possible that, if woman suffrage is agitated as a means of removing these evils, the effect may be to prolong their existence?[43]

Characteristically, she added that she had no time to work on suffrage and she made it a practice never to give her name where she could not give her work. She ended her letter to Mill with a request that he aid her in her work—Indian sanitary reform! Once Mill made it clear to her that her name alone was valuable, she joined the organization and was a dues-paying member for years.

Florence Nightingale continued to perform staggering amounts of work for the rest of her long life. That any of her colleagues should desire a personal life enraged her. When her Aunt Mai, who had accompanied her to the Crimea and remained with her afterward, wanted to return home to visit her own family, Nightingale broke with her for twenty years. She refused to recognize, when Sidney Herbert was dying, that work was beyond his capacities. When Mary Clarke paid a rare visit to England, Nightingale would not interrupt her daily schedule of work for even a brief visit! Everything was rooted out of her life but her work—her papers, her statistics, her reports. Nothing personal, certainly nothing political remained; and her vision, as a result, suffered a narrowing. After "Cassandra," Nightingale turned away from the subject of the condition of women. As a Victorian recluse dedicated only to work, she lost sight of the crippling disabilities—economic, social, educational, political—under which most women continued to suffer; and she failed to understand the necessary work of support, of education, of raising public awareness, in which the women's movement of her time was engaged.

Florence Nightingale belongs with what Ray Strachey, in *The Cause,* calls the first wave of women, who early in the nineteenth century entered philanthropic work—with Louisa Twining, whose efforts centered on workhouses, and Mary Carpenter, a pioneer in reformatories and "ragged schools."[44] Their focus initially was on getting the work done. Only gradually did some of them become aware of the implications of their work for the lives of women.

Nevertheless, the contribution Florence Nightingale made to the advancement of women cannot be dismissed: she enlarged the world's view of women's capabilities and created a respectable, well paid, highly trained profession for women. This contribution was recognized more clearly in her own day than it has been in ours. Lord Stanley, for example, commented:

Mark what, by breaking through customs and prejudice, Miss Nightingale has effected for her sex. She has opened to them a new profession, a new sphere of usefulness. ... a claim for more extended freedom of action. I do not suppose that in undertaking her mission, she thought much of the effect which it might have on the social position of women. Yet probably no one of those who made that question a special study has done half as much as she towards its settlement.[45]

She was recognized in her own time and must certainly be recognized now for the valuable role she played in what the historian Wanda Neff has called "the revolt of the idle woman" in the 1850s, the movement to train, employ, and free women.[46]

What rings truest in Florence Nightingale's life, what emerges most strongly from "Cassandra," is her belief in the necessity for women to take their lives as seriously as men take theirs—to train themselves for work and to do that work wholeheartedly. And she saw clearly that domestic obligations made this difficult if not impossible, that the home and family all too often prevented women from developing their capabilities and putting them to use. In these insights, in her work, and in her criticism of the condition of women in "Cassandra," Florence Nightingale is a significant figure in the great feminist thrust of the nineteenth century.

[1]Sir Edward Cook, *The Life of Florence Nightingale*, 2 vols. (London, 1913), I, 64. She was, of course, *Miss* Nightingale. The newspaper's error is most revealing.

[2]Ibid., I, 234.

[3]Lytton Strachey, *Eminent Victorians* (New York, 1918), p. 160.

[4]Cook, I, 314.

[5]Cecil Woodham-Smith, *Florence Nightingale* (New York, 1951), p. 266.

[6]Lytton Strachey, p. 185.

[7]Victorian working women are discussed in Wanda Fraiken Neff, *Victorian Working Women:An Historical and Literary Study of Women in British Industries and Professions,1832-1850* (New York, 1929); in Ivy Pinchbeck, *Women Workers and the Industrial Revolution,1750-1850* (New York, 1969); in Margaret Hewitt, *Wives and Mothers in Victorian Industry* (London, 1958); in Lee Holcombe, *Victorian Ladies at Work:Middle Class Working Women in England and Wales, 1850-1914* (Newton Abbot, 1973); and in books dealing with the life of the middle and upper class Victorian woman.

[8]Ironically, as low as the wages were, the money meant freedom from the family for the young, single, working woman.

[9]Martha Vicinus, *Suffer and Be Still:Women in the Victorian Age* (Bloomington, Indiana, 1972), Introduction, xi. The life of the middle- and upper-class Victorian woman is discussed in this book; in Duncan Crow, *The Victorian Woman* (New York, 1972); in Françoise Basch, *Relative Creatures: Victorian Women in Society and the Novel* (New York, 1974); and most recently in Patricia Branca, *Silent Sisterhood: Middle Class Women in the Victorian Home* (Pittsburgh, 1975), a book which critically examines many accepted beliefs about Victorian middle-class women and credits them with a more active role in family life than formerly believed. Although Branca argues that the middle-class woman was less passive and idle than was thought, she agrees that the Victorian middle-class family typically had at least one servant, often more.

[10]Vicinus, p. ix.

[11]Woodham-Smith, p. 25.

[12]Ibid., p. 43.

[13]Crow, p. 204.

[14]Woodham-Smith, p. 9.

[15]Cook, I, 106.

[16]Woodham-Smith, p. 162.

[17]Ibid., p. 20.

[18]Ibid., p. 46.

[19]Even as a young child, she thought that she was different from those around her; she recorded in a private note her belief that she was a monster, incapable of behaving like others (Woodham-Smith, p. 6).

[20]Ibid., pp. 58-59.

[21]Ibid., p. 12.

[22]Ibid., p. 13. These were: the first "call" in 1837; the second before she assumed her first position—in Harley Street, London, at the Hospital for Poor Gentlewomen; the next immediately before the Crimea; and the last after Sidney Herbert's death, when she realized that she would have to carry on the work of reform without him.

[23]Ibid., p. 62.

[24]Ibid., p. 28.

[25]Woodham-Smith, p. 51.

[26]Ibid., p. 52.

[27]Cook, I, 102.

[28]Woodham-Smith, p. 44.

[29]Lytton Strachey, p. 134.

[30]Woodham-Smith, p. 58.

[31]Ibid., p. 63.

[32]Cook, I, 117.

[33]Ibid., I, 122.

[34]Virginia Woolf, *A Room of One's Own* (New York, 1957), p. 57. Referring to earlier generations of women, Woolf says, "Among your grandmothers and great-grandmothers there were many that wept their eyes out. Florence Nightingale shrieked aloud in her agony." Her footnote reads, "See *Cassandra*, by Florence Nightingale."

[35]"Cassandra" is, as Lytton Strachey called it, an intensely personal "cri du coeur" (p. 189). Indeed there are some references in Florence Nightingale's letters and notes to herself as Cassandra. "Poor Cassandra," she writes after a dinner party in the days when she was trying to convince her parents to let her train as a nurse, "has found an unexpected ally in a young surgeon of a London hospital" (Cook, I, 116-17). The name Cassandra may very well have been the name of the heroine of her proposed novel. It is, however, a very well chosen name

apart from its personal applications. Cassandra was the prophetess cursed by Apollo so that she was doomed to see and speak the truth, but never to be believed.

Florence Nightingale submitted *Suggestions For Thought* to John Stuart Mill and to Benjamin Jowett, the classical scholar and a close friend. Mill urged her to publish; Jowett felt the volumes were disorganized and needed revision. Sir Edward Cook (I, 471) notes the influence of "Cassandra" on Mill's *The Subjection of Women*, which alludes to "a celebrated woman, in a work which I hope will someday be published. . . ."

[36]Woodham-Smith, p. 260.

[37]Cook, I, 385.

[38]Woodham-Smith, p. 306.

[39]Ibid., p. 259.

[40]Ibid., p. 199.

[41]Sir George Pickering, *Creative Malady* (New York, 1974), p. 165.

[42]Cook, II, 404.

[43]Cook, II, 216.

[44]Rachel Strachey, Chapter V, "Setting to Work."

[45]Cook, I, 305.

[46]Neff, p. 242.

Chronology
of the Life of Florence Nightingale

May 12, 1820: Birth of Florence Nightingale, Florence, Italy.

1839: Meets Mary Clarke in Paris.

1850: First visit to Kaiserwerth.

1852: Begins training at Kaiserwerth.

1852: Writes "Cassandra."

1853: Receives an allowance of 500 pounds a year from her father and takes a place of her own in London.

1853: Assumes duties of Superintendent of Hospital for Invalid Gentlewomen, Harley Street, London.

1854–1856: Works in the Crimea.

1855: The Nightingale Fund formed.

1860: Establishes the Nightingale School and Home for Nurses at St. Thomas's Hospital, London, with capital provided from the Nightingale Fund.

1860: Publishes *Notes on Nursing; What It Is and What It Is Not.*

1860: "Suggestions For Thought to the Searchers After Truth Among the Artizans of England," privately printed.

1861: Establishes the Training School for Midwives at King's College Hospital, London, with capital provided from the Nightingale Fund.

1865: Moves to South Street, London, where she works unceasingly until well into her eighties.

1907: Awarded the Order of Merit.

August 13, 1910: Death of Florence Nightingale.

Cassandra

By Florence Nightingale

I

"The voice of one crying in the" crowd,
"Prepare ye the way of the Lord."

ONE OFTEN COMES to be thus wandering alone in the bitterness of life without. It might be that such an one might be tempted to seek an escape in hope of a more congenial sphere. Yet, perhaps, if prematurely we dismiss ourselves from this world, all may even have to be suffered through again—the premature birth may not contribute to the production of another being, which must be begun again from the beginning.

Such an one longs to replunge into the happy unconscious sleep of the rest of the race! they slumber in one another's arms—they are not yet awake. To them evil and suffering are not, for they are not conscious of evil. While one alone, awake and prematurely alive to it, must wander out in silence and solitude—such an one has awakened too early, has risen up too soon, has rejected the companionship of the race, unlinked to any human being. Such an one sees the evil they do not see, and yet has no power to discover the remedy for it.

Why have women passion, intellect, moral activity—these three—and a place in society where no one of the three can be exercised? Men say that God punishes for complaining. No, but men are angry with misery. They are irritated with women for not being happy. They take it as a personal offence. To God alone may women complain, without insulting Him!

And women, who are afraid, while in words they acknowledge that God's work is good, to say, Thy will be *not* done (declaring another order of society from that which He has made), go about maudling to each other and teaching to their daughters that "women have no passions." In the conventional society, which men have made for women, and women have accepted, they *must* have none, they *must* act the farce of hypocrisy, the lie that they are without passion— and therefore what else can they say to their daughters, without giving the lie to themselves?

"Suffering, sad" female "humanity!" What are these feelings which they are taught to consider as disgraceful, to deny to themselves? What form do the Chinese feet assume when denied their proper development? If the young girls of the "higher classes," who never commit a false step, whose justly earned reputations were never sullied even by the stain which the fruit of mere "knowledge of good and evil" leaves behind, were to speak, and say what are their thoughts employed upon, their *thoughts*, which alone are free, what would they say?

That, with the phantom companion of their fancy, they talk (not love, they are too innocent, too pure, too full of genius and imagination for that, but) they talk, in fancy, of that which interests them most; they seek a companion for their every thought; the companion they find not in reality they seek in fancy, or, if not that, if not absorbed in endless conversations, they see themselves engaged with him in stirring events, circumstances which call out the interest wanting to them. Yes, fathers, mothers, you who see your daughter proudly rejecting all semblance of flirtation, primly engaged in the duties of the breakfast table, you little think how her fancy compensates itself by endless interviews and sympathies (sympathies either for ideas or events) with the fancy's companion of the hour! And you say, "She is not susceptible. Women have no passion." Mothers, who cradle yourselves in visions about the domestic hearth, how many of your sons and daughters are *there*, do you think, while sitting round under your complacent maternal eye? Were you there yourself during your own (now forgotten) girlhood?

What are the thoughts of these young girls while one is singing Schubert, another is reading the Review, and a third is busy embroidering? Is not one fancying herself the nurse of some new friend in sickness; another engaging in romantic dangers with him, such as call out the character and afford more food for sympathy than the monotonous events of domestic society; another undergoing unheard-of trials under the observation of someone whom she has chosen as the companion of her dream? another having a loving and loved companion in the life she is living, which many do not want to change?

And is not all this most natural, inevitable? Are they, who are too much ashamed of it to confess it even to themselves, to be blamed for that which cannot be otherwise, the causes of which stare one in the face, *if one's eyes were not closed?* Many struggle against this as a "snare." No Trappist ascetic watches or fasts more in the body than these do in the soul! They understand the discipline of Thebaïd—the life-long agonies to which those strong moral Mohicans subjected themselves. How cordially they could do the same, in order to escape the worse torture of wandering "vain imaginations." But the laws of God for moral well-being are not thus to be obeyed. We fast mentally, scourge ourselves morally, use the intellectual hair-shirt, in order to subdue the perpetual day-dreaming, which is so dangerous! We resolve "this day month I will be free from it;" twice a day with

27

prayer and written record of the times when we have indulged in it, we endeavour to combat it. Never, with the slightest success. By mortifying vanity we do ourselves no good. It is the want of interest in our life which produces it; by filling up that want of interest in our life we can alone remedy it. And, did we even see this, how can we make the difference? How obtain the interest which Society declares *she* does not want, and *we* cannot want?

What are novels? What is the secret of the charm of every romance that ever was written? The first thing in a good novel is to place the persons together in circumstances which naturally call out the high feelings and thoughts of the character, which afford food for sympathy between them on these points—romantic events they are called. The second is that the heroine has *generally* no family ties (almost *invariably* no mother), or, if she has, these do not interfere with her entire independence.

These two things constitute the main charm of reading novels. Now, in as far as these are good and not spurious interests, let us see what we have to correspond with them in real life. Can high sympathies be fed upon the opera, the exhibitions, the gossip of the House of Commons, and the political caricature? If, together, man and woman approach any of the high questions of social, political, or religious life, they are said (and justly—under our present disqualifications) to be going "too far." That such things can be!

"Is it Thou, Lord?" And He said, "It is I." Let our hearts be still.

II

"Yet I would spare no pang,
Would wish no torture less,
The more that anguish racks,
The earlier it will bless."

GIVE US BACK our suffering, we cry to Heaven in our hearts —suffering rather than indifferentism; for out of nothing comes nothing. But out of suffering may come the cure. Better have pain than paralysis! A hundred struggle and drown in the breakers. One discovers the new world. But rather, ten times rather, die in the surf, heralding the way to that new world, than stand idly on the shore!

Passion, intellect, moral activity—these three have never been satisfied in woman. In this cold and oppressive conventional atmosphere, they cannot be satisfied. To say more on this subject would be to enter into the whole history of society, of the present state of civilization.

Look at that lizard—"It is not hot," he says, "I like it. The atmosphere which enervates you is life to me." The state of society which some complain of makes others happy. Why should these complain to those? *They* do not suffer. *They* would not understand it, any more than that lizard would comprehend the sufferings of a Shetland sheep.

The progressive world is necessarily divided into two classes—those who take the best of what there is and enjoy it—those who wish for something better and try to create it. Without these two classes, the world would be badly off. They are the very conditions of progress, both the one and the other. Were there none who were discontented with what they have, the world would never reach anything better. And, through the other class, which is constantly taking the best of what the first is creating for them, a balance is secured, and that which is conquered is held fast. But with neither class must we quarrel for not possessing the privileges of the other. The laws of the nature of each make it impossible.

Is discontent a privilege?

Yes, it is a privilege to suffer for your race—a privilege not reserved to the Redeemer and the martyrs alone, but one enjoyed by numbers in every age.

The common-place lives of thousands; and in that is its only interest—its only merit as a history: vis., that it *is* the type of common sufferings—the story of one who has not the courage to resist nor to submit to the civilization of her time—is this.

Poetry and imagination begin life. A child will fall on its knees on the gravel walk at the sight of a pink hawthorn in full flower, when it is by itself, to praise God for it.

Then comes intellect. It wishes to satisfy the wants which intellect creates for it. But there is a physical, not moral, impossibility of supplying the wants of the intellect in the state of civilization at which we have arrived. The stimulus, the training, the time, are all three wanting to us; or, in other words, the means and inducements are not there.

Look at the poor lives which we lead. It is a wonder that we are so good as we are, not that we are so bad. In looking round we are struck with the power of the organizations we see, not with their want of power. Now and then, it is true, we are conscious that *there* is an inferior organization, but, in general, just the contrary. Mrs. A. has the imagination, the poetry of a Murillo, and has sufficient power of execution to show that she might have had a great deal more. Why is she not a Murillo? From a material difficulty, not a mental one. If she has a knife and fork in her hands during three hours of the day, she cannot have a pencil or brush. Dinner is the great sacred ceremony of this day, the great sacrament. To be absent from dinner is equivalent to being ill. Nothing else will excuse us from it. Bodily incapacity is the only apology valid. If she has a pen and ink in her hands during other three hours, writing answers for the penny post; again, she cannot have her pencil, and so *ad infinitum* through life. People have no type before them in their lives, neither fathers and mothers, nor the children themselves. They look at things in detail. They say, "It is very desirable that A., my daughter, should go to such a party, should know such a lady, should sit by such a person." It is true. But what standard have they before them? of the nature and destination of man? The very words are rejected as pedantic. But might they not, at least, have a type in their minds that such an one might be a discoverer through her intellect, such another through her art, a third through her moral power?

Women often try one branch of intellect after another in their youth, *e.g.,* mathematics. But that, least of all, is compatible with the life of "society." It is impossible to follow up anything systematically. Women often long to enter some man's profession where they would find direction, competition (or rather opportunity of measuring the intellect with others), and, above all, time.

In those wise institutions, mixed as they are with many follies, which will last as long as the human race lasts, because they are adapted to the wants of the human race; those institutions which we call monasteries, and which, embracing much that is contrary to the laws of nature, are yet better adapted to the union of the life of action and that of thought than any other mode of life with which we are acquainted; in many such, four and a half hours, at least, are daily set aside for thought, rules are given for thought, training and opportunity afforded. Among us, there is *no* time appointed for this purpose, and the difficulty is that, in our social life, we must be always doubtful whether we ought not to be with somebody else or be doing something else.

Are men better off than women in this?

If one calls upon a friend in London and sees her son in the drawing-room, it strikes one as odd to find a young man sitting idling in his mother's drawing-room in the morning. For men, who are seen much in those haunts, there is no end of the epithets we have; "knights of the carpet," "drawing-room heroes," "ladies' men." But suppose we were to see a number of men in the morning sitting round a table in the drawing-room, looking at prints, doing worsted work, and reading little books, how we should laugh! A member of the House of Commons was once known to do worsted work. Of another man was said, "His only fault is that he is too good; he drives out with his mother every day in the carriage, and if he is asked anywhere he answers that he must dine with his mother, but, if she can spare him, he will come in to tea, and he does not come."

Now, why is it more ridiculous for a man than for a woman to do worsted work and drive out every day in the carriage? Why should we laugh if we were to see a parcel of men sitting round a drawing-room table in the morning, and think it all right if they were women?

Is man's time more valuable than woman's? or is the difference between man and woman this, that woman has confessedly nothing to do?

Women are never supposed to have any occupation of sufficient importance *not* to be interrupted, except "suckling their fools;" and women themselves have accepted this, have written books to support it, and have trained themselves so as to consider whatever they do as *not* of such value to the world or to others, but that they can throw it up at the first "claim of social life." They have accustomed themselves to consider intellectual occupation as a merely selfish amusement, which it is their "duty" to give up for every trifler more selfish than themselves.

A young man (who was afterwards useful and known in his day and generation) when busy reading and sent for by his proud mother to shine in some morning visit, came; but, after it was over, he said, "Now, remember, this is not to happen again. I came that you might not think me sulky, but I shall not come again." But for a young woman to send such a message to her mother and sisters, how impertinent it would be! A woman of great administrative powers said that she never undertook anything which she "could not throw by at once, if necessary."

How do we explain then the many cases of women who have distinguished themselves in classics, mathematics, even in politics?

Widowhood, ill-health, or want of bread, these three explanations or excuses are supposed to justify a woman in taking up an occupation. In some cases, no doubt, an indomitable force of character will suffice without any of these three, but such are rare.

But see how society fritters away the intellects of those committed to her charge! It is said that society is necessary to sharpen the intellect. But what do we seek society for? It does sharpen the intellect, because it is a kind of *tour-de-force* to say something at a pinch—unprepared and uninterested with any subject, to improvise something under difficulties. But what "go we out for to seek?" To take the chance of some one having something to say which we want to hear? or of our finding something to say which *they* want to hear? You have a little to say, but not much. You often make a stipulation with some one else, "Come in ten minutes, for I shall not be able to find enough to spin out longer than that." You are not to talk of anything very interesting, for the essence of society is to prevent any long conversations and all *tête-à-têtes*. "Glissez, n'appuyez pas" is its very motto. The praise of a good "*maîtresse de maison*" consists in this, that she allows no one person to be too much absorbed in, or too long about, a conversation. She always recalls them to their "duty." People do not go into the company of their fellow-creatures for what would seem a very sufficient reason, namely, that they have something to say to them, or something that they want to hear from them; but in the vague hope that they may find something to say.

Then as to solitary opportunities. Women never have half an hour in all their lives (excepting before or after anybody is up in the house) that they can call their own, without fear of offending or of hurting some one. Why do people sit up so late, or, more rarely, get up so early? Not because the day is not long enough, but because they have "no time in the day to themselves."

If we do attempt to do anything in company, what is the system of literary exercise which we pursue? Everybody reads aloud out of their own book or newspaper—or, every five minutes, something is said. And what is it to be "read aloud to?" The most miserable exercise of the human intellect. Or rather, is it any exercise at all? It is like lying on one's back, with one's hands tied and having liquid poured down one's throat. Worse than that, because suffocation would immediately ensue and put a stop to this operation. But no suffocation would stop the other.

So much for the satisfaction of the intellect. Yet for a married woman in society, it is even worse. A married woman was heard to wish that she could break a limb that she might have a little time to herself. Many take advantage of the fear of "infection" to do the same.

It is a thing *so* accepted among women that they have nothing to do, that one woman has not the least scruple in saying to another, "I will come and spend the morning with you." And you would be thought quite surly and absurd, if you were to refuse it on the plea of occupation. Nay, it is thought a mark of amiability and affection, if you are "on such terms" that you can "come in" "any morning you please."

In a country house, if there is a large party of young people, "You will spend the morning with us," they say to the neighbours, "we will drive together in the afternoon," "tomorrow we will make an expedition, and we will spend the evening together." And this is thought friendly, and spending time in a pleasant manner. So women play through life. Yet time is the most valuable of all things. If they had come every morning and afternoon and robbed us of half-a-crown we should have had redress from the police. But it is laid down, that our time is of no value. If you offer a morning visit to a professional man, and say, "I will just stay an hour with you, if you will allow me, till so and so comes back to fetch me;" it costs him the earnings of an hour, and therefore he has a right to complain. But women have no right, because it is "*only* their time."

Women have no means given them, whereby they *can* resist the "claims of social life." They are taught from their infancy upwards that it is wrong, ill-tempered, and a misunderstanding of "a woman's mission" (with a great M.) if they do not allow themselves *willingly* to be interrupted at all hours. If a woman has once put in a claim to be treated as a man by some work of science or art or literature, which she can *show* as the "fruit of her leisure," then she will be considered justified in *having* leisure (hardly, perhaps, even then). But if not, not. If she has nothing to show, she must resign herself to her fate.

III

I LIKE RIDING ABOUT this beautiful place, why don't you? I like walking about the garden, why don't you?" is the common expostulation—as if we were children, whose spirits rise during a fortnight's holidays, who think that they will last for ever—and look neither backwards nor forwards.

Society triumphs over many. They wish to regenerate the world with their institutions, with their moral philosophy, with their love. Then they sink to living from breakfast till dinner, from dinner till tea, with a little worsted work, and to looking forward to nothing but bed.

When shall we see a life full of steady enthusiasm, walking straight to its aim, flying home, as that bird is now, against the wind—with the calmness and the confidence of one who knows the laws of God and can apply them?

What *do* we see? We see great and fine organizations deteriorating. We see girls and boys of seventeen, before whose noble ambitions, heroic dreams, and rich endowments we bow our heads, as before *God incarnate in the flesh.* But, ere they are thirty, they are withered, paralysed, extinguished. "We have forgotten our visions," they say themselves.

The "dreams of youth" have become a proverb. That organizations, early rich, fall far short of their promise has been repeated to satiety. But is it extraordinary that it should be so? For do we ever *utilize* this heroism? Look how it lives upon itself and perishes for lack of food. We do not know what to do with it. We had rather that it should not be there. Often we laugh at it. Always we find it troublesome. Look at the poverty of our life! Can we expect anything else but poor creatures to come out of it? Did Michael Angelo's genius fail, did Pascal's die in its bud, did Sir Isaac Newton become a common-place sort of man? In two of these cases the knife wore out the sheath. But the knife itself did not become rusty, till the body was dead or infirm.

Why cannot we *make use* of the noble rising heroisms of our own day, instead of leaving them to rust?

They have nothing to do.

Are they to be employed in sitting in the drawing-room, saying words which may as well not be said, which could be said as well if *they* were not there?

Women often strive to live by intellect. The clear, brilliant, sharp radiance of intellect's moonlight rising upon such an expanse of snow is dreary, it is true, but some love its solemn desolation, its silence, its solitude—if they are but *allowed* to live in it; if they are not perpetually baulked and disappointed. But a woman cannot live in the light of intellect. Society forbids it. Those conventional frivolities, which are called her "duties," forbid it. Her "domestic duties," high-sounding words, which, for the most part, are but bad habits (which she has not the courage to enfranchise herself from, the strength to break through) forbid it. What are these duties (or bad habits)?—Answering a multitude of letters which lead to nothing, from her so-called friends— keeping herself up to the level of the world that she may furnish her quota of amusement at the breakfast-table; driving out her company in the carriage. And all these things are exacted from her by her family which, if she is good and affectionate, will have more influence with her than the world.

What wonder if, wearied out, sick at heart with hope deferred, the springs of will broken, not seeing clearly *where* her duty lies, she abandons intellect as a vocation and takes it only, as we use the moon, by glimpses through her tight-closed window-shutters?

The family? It is too narrow a field for the development of an immortal spirit, be that spirit male or female. The chances are a thousand to one that, in that small sphere, the task for which that immortal spirit is destined by the qualities and the gifts which its Creator has placed within it, will not be found.

The family uses people, *not* for what they are, not for what they are intended to be, but for what it wants them for —for its own uses. It thinks of them not as what God has made them, but as the something which *it* has arranged that they shall be. If it wants some one to sit in the drawing-room, *that* some one is to be supplied by the family, though that member may be destined for science, or for education, or for active superintendence by God, *i.e.,* by the gifts within.

This system dooms some minds to incurable infancy, others to silent misery.

And family boasts that it has performed its mission well, in as far as it has enabled the individual to say, "I have *no* peculiar work, nothing but what the moment brings me, nothing that I cannot throw up at once at anybody's claim;" in as far, that is, as it has *destroyed* the individual life. And the individual thinks that a great victory has been accomplished, when, at last, she is able to say that she has "no personal desires or plans." What is this but throwing the gifts of God aside as worthless, and substituting for them those of the world?

Marriage is the only chance (and it is but a chance) offered to women for escape from this death; and how eagerly and how ignorantly it is embraced!

At present we live to impede each other's satisfactions; competition, domestic life, society, what is it all but this? We go somewhere where we are not wanted and where we don't want to go. What else is conventional life? *Passivity* when we want to be active. So many hours spent every day in passively doing what conventional life tells us, when we would so gladly be at work.

And is it a wonder that all individual life is extinguished?

Women dream of a great sphere of steady, not sketchy benevolence, of moral activity, for which they would fain be trained and fitted, instead of working in the dark, neither knowing nor registering whither their steps lead, whether farther from or nearer to the aim.

For how do people exercise their moral activity now? We visit, we teach, we talk, among "the poor;" we are told, "don't look for the fruits, cast thy bread upon the waters: for thou shalt find it after many days." Certainly "don't look," for you won't see. You will *not* "find it," and then you would "strike work."

How different would be the heart for the work, and how different would be the success, if we learnt our work as a serious study, and followed it out steadily as a profession!

Were the physician to set to work at *his* trade, as the

philanthropist does at his, how many bodies would he not spoil before he cured one!

We set the treatment of bodies so high above the treatment of souls, that the physician occupies a higher place in society than the schoolmaster. The governess is to have every one of God's gifts; she is to do that which the mother herself is incapable of doing; but our son must not degrade himself by marrying the governess, nor our daughter the tutor, though she might marry the medical man.

But my medical man does do something for me, it is said, my tutor has done nothing.

This is true, this is the real reason. And what a condemnation of the state of mental science it is! Low as is physical science, that of the mind is still lower.

Women long for an education to teach them *to teach*, to teach them the laws of the human mind and how to apply them—and knowing how imperfect, in the present state of the world, such an education must be, they long for experience, not patch-work experience, but experience followed up and systematized, to enable them to know what they are about and *where* they are "casting their bread" and whether it *is "bread"* or a stone.

How should we learn a language if we were to give to it an hour a week? A fortnight's steady application would make more way in it than a year of such patch-work. A "lady" can hardly go to "her school" two days running. She cannot leave the breakfast-table—or she must be fulfilling some little frivolous "duty," which others ought not to exact, or which might just as well be done some other time.

Dreaming always—never accomplishing; thus women live —too much ashamed of their dreams, which they think "romantic," to tell them where they will be laughed at, even if not considered wrong.

With greater strength of purpose they might accomplish something. But if they were strong, all of them, they would not need to have their story told, for all the world would read it in the mission they have fulfilled. It is for common place, every-day characters that we tell our tale—because it is the sample of hundreds of lives (or rather deaths) of persons who cannot fight with society, or who, unsupported by the sympathies about them, give up their own destiny as not worth the fierce and continued struggle necessary to accomplish it. *One* struggle they *could* make and be free (and, in the Church of Rome, many, many, unallured by any other motive, make this one struggle to enter a convent); but the perpetual series of petty spars, with discouragements between, and doubts as to whether they are right—these wear out the very life necessary to make them.

If a man were to follow up his profession or occupation at odd times, how would he do it? Would he become skilful in that profession? It is acknowledged by women themselves that they are inferior in every occupation to men. Is it wonderful? *They* do *everything* at "odd times."

And if a woman's music and drawing are only used by her as an amusement (a *pass-time*, as it is called), is it wonderful that she tires of them, that she becomes disgusted with them?

In every dream of the life of intelligence or that of activity, women are accompanied by a phantom—the phantom of sympathy, guiding, lighting the way—even if they do not marry. Some few sacrifice marriage, because they must sacrifice all other life if they accept that. That man and woman have an equality of duties and rights is accepted by woman even less than by man. Behind *his* destiny woman must annihilate herself, must be only his complement. A woman dedicates herself to the vocation of her husband; she fills up and performs the subordinate parts in it. But if she has any destiny, any vocation of her own, she must renounce it, in nine cases out of ten. Some few, like Mrs. Somerville, Mrs. Chisholm, Mrs. Fry, have not done so; but these are exceptions. The fact is that woman has so seldom any vocation of her own, that it does not much signify; she has none to renounce. A man gains everything by marriage: he gains a "helpmate," but a woman does not.

But if ever women come into contact with sickness, and crime, and poverty in masses, how the practical reality of life revives them! They are exhausted, like those who live on opium or on novels, all their lives—exhausted with feelings which lead to no action. If they see and enter into a continuous line of action, with a full and interesting life, with training constantly kept up to the occupation, occupation constantly testing the training—it is the *beau-idéal* of practical, not theoretical, education—they are re-tempered, their life is filled, they have found their work, and the means to do it.

Women, while they are young, sometimes think that an actress's life is a happy one—not for the sake of the admiration, not for the sake of the fame; but because in the morning she studies, in the evening she embodies those studies: she has the means of testing and correcting them by practice, and of resuming her studies in the morning, to improve the weak parts, remedy the failures, and in the evening try the corrections again. It is, indeed, true that, even after middle age, with such exercise of faculty, there is no end to the progress which may be made.

Some are only deterred from suicide because it is in the most distinct manner to say to God: "I will not, I will not do as Thou wouldst have me," and because it is "no use."

To have no food for our heads, no food for our hearts, no food for our activity, is that nothing? If we have no food for the body, how we do cry out, how all the world hears of it, how all the newspapers talk of it, with a paragraph headed in great capital letters, DEATH FROM STARVATION! But suppose one were to put a paragraph in the "Times," *Death of Thought from Starvation*, or *Death of Moral Activity from Starvation*, how people would stare, how they would laugh and wonder! One would think we had no heads or hearts, by the total indifference of the public towards them. Our bodies are the only things of any consequence.

We have nothing to do which raises us, no food which agrees with us. We can never pursue any object for a single two hours, for we can never command any regular leisure or solitude; and in social or domestic life one is bound, under pain of being thought sulky, to make a remark every two minutes.

Men are on the side of society; they blow hot and cold; they say, "Why can't you employ yourself in society?" and then, "Why don't you talk in society?" I can pursue a connected conversation, or I can be silent; but to drop a remark, as it is called, every two minutes, how wearisome it is! It is impossible to pursue the current of one's own thoughts, because one must keep oneself ever on the alert "to say something;" and it is impossible to say what one is thinking, because the essence of a remark is not to be a thought, but an impression. With what labour women have toiled to break down all individual and independent life, in order to fit themselves for this social and domestic existence, thinking it right! And when they have killed themselves to do it, they have awakened (too late) to think it wrong.

For, later in life, women could not make use of leisure and solitude if they had it! Like the Chinese woman, who could not make use of her feet, if she were brought into European life.

Some have an attention like a battering-ram, which, slowly brought to bear, can work upon a subject for any length of time. They can work ten hours just as well as two upon the same thing. But this age would have men like the musket, which you can load so fast that nothing but its heating in the process puts any limit to the number and frequency of times of firing, and at as many different objects as you please.

So, later in life, people cannot use their battering-ram. Their attention, like society's, goes off in a thousand different directions. They are an hour before they can fix it; and by the time it is fixed, the leisure is gone. They become incapable of consecutive or strenuous work.

What these suffer—even physically—from the want of such work no one can tell. The accumulation of nervous energy, which has had nothing to do during the day, makes them feel every night, when they go to bed, as if they were going mad; and they are obliged to lie long in bed in the morning to let it evaporate and keep it down.

At last they suffer at once from disgust of the one and incapacity for the other—from loathing of conventional idleness and powerlessness to do work when they have it. "Now go, you have several hours," say people, "you have all the afternoon to yourself." When they are all frittered away, they are to begin to work. When they are broken up into little bits, they are to hew away.

IV

MORAL ACTIVITY? There is scarcely such a thing possible! Everything is sketchy. The world does nothing but sketch. One Lady Bountiful sketches a school, but it never comes to a finished study; she can hardly work at it two weeks consecutively. Here and there a solitary individual, it is true, makes a really careful study,—as Mrs. Chisholm of emigration—as Miss Carpenter of reformatory discipline. But, in general, a "lady" has too many sketches on hand. She has a sketch of society, a sketch of her children's education, sketches of her "charities," sketches of her reading. She is like a painter who should have five pictures in his studio at once, and giving now a stroke to one, and now a stroke to another, till he had made the whole round, should continue this routine to the end.

All life is sketchy,—the poet's verse (compare Tennyson, Milnes, and Mrs. Browning with Milton or even Byron: it is not the difference of genius which strikes one so much as the unfinished state of these modern sketches compared with the studies of the old masters),—the artist's picture, the author's composition—all are rough, imperfect, incomplete, even as works of art.

And how can it be otherwise? A "leader" out of a newspaper, an article out of a review, five books read aloud in the course of an evening, such is our literature. What mind can stand three leading articles every morning as its food?

When shall we see a woman making a *study* of what she does? Married women cannot; for a man would think, if his wife undertook any great work with the intention of carrying it out,—of making anything but a sham of it—that she would "suckle his fools and chronicle his small beer" less well for it,—that he would not have so good a dinner—that she would destroy, as it is called, his domestic life.

The intercourse of man and woman—how frivolous, how unworthy it is! Can we call *that* the true vocation of woman —her high career? Look round at the marriages which you know. The true marriage—that noble union, by which a man and woman become together the one perfect being— probably does not exist at present upon earth.

It is not surprising that husbands and wives seem so little part of one another. It is surprising that there is so much love as there is. For there is no food for it. What does it live upon —what nourishes it? Husbands and wives never seem to have anything to say to one another. What do they talk about? Not about any great religious, social, political questions or feelings. They talk about who shall come to dinner, who is to live in this lodge and who in that, about the improvement of the place, or when they shall go to London. If there are children, they form a common subject of some nourishment. But, even then, the case is oftenest thus,—the husband is to think of how they are to get on in life; the wife of bringing them up at home.

But any real communion between husband and wife—any descending into the depths of their being, and drawing out thence what they find and comparing it—do we ever dream of such a thing? Yes, we may dream of it during the season of "passion;" but we shall not find it afterwards. We even *expect* it to go off, and lay our account that it will. If the husband has, by chance, gone into the depths of *his* being, and found anything there unorthodox, he, oftenest, conceals it carefully from his wife,—he is afraid of "unsettling her opinions."

What is the mystery of passion, spiritually speaking? For there *is* a passion of the Spirit. *Blind* passion, as it has most truly been called, seems to come on in man without his exactly knowing why, without his *at all* knowing why for *this* person rather than for *that*, and (whether it has been satisfied or unsatisfied) to go off again after a while, as it came, also without his knowing why.

The woman's passion is generally more lasting.

It is possible that this difference may be, because there is really more in man than in woman. There is nothing in her for him to have this intimate communion *with*. He cannot impart to her his religious beliefs, if he have any, because she would be "shocked." Religious men are and must be heretics now—for we must not pray, except in a "form" of words, made beforehand—or think of God but with a pre-arranged idea.

With the man's political ideas, if they extend beyond the merest party politics, she has no sympathy.

His social ideas, if they are "advanced," she will probably denounce without knowing why, as savouring of "socialism" (a convenient word, which covers a multitude of new ideas and offences). For woman is "by birth a Tory,"—has been often said—by education a "Tory," we mean.

Woman has nothing but her affections,—and this makes her at once more loving and less loved.

But is it suprising that there should be so little real marriage, when we think what the process is which leads to marriage?

Under the eyes of an always present mother and sisters (of whom even the most refined and intellectual cannot abstain from a jest upon the subject, who think it their *duty* to be anxious, to watch every germ and bud of it) the acquaintance begins. It is fed—upon what?—the gossip of art, musical and pictorial, the party politics of the day, the chit-chat of society, and people marry or sometimes they don't marry, discouraged by the impossibility of knowing any more of one another than this will furnish.

They prefer to marry in *thought*, to hold imaginary conversations with one another in idea, rather than, on such a flimsy pretext of communion, to take the chance (*certainly* it cannot be) of having more to say to one another in marriage.

Men and women meet now *to be idle*. Is it extraordinary that they do not know each other, and that, in their mutual ignorance, they form no surer friendships? Did they meet to *do* something together, then indeed they might form some real tie.

But, as it is, *they* are not there, it is only a mask which is there—a mouth-piece of ready-made sentences about the "topics of the day;" and then people rail against men for choosing a woman "for her face"—why, what else do they see?

It is very well to say "be prudent, be careful, try to know each other." But how are you to know each other?

Unless a woman has lost all pride, how is it possible for her, under the eyes of all her family, to indulge in long exclusive conversations with a man? "Such a thing" must not take place till after her "engagement." And how is she to make an engagement, if "such a thing" has not taken place?

Besides, young women at home have so little to occupy and to interest them—they have so little reason for *not* quitting their home, that a young and independent man cannot look at a girl without giving rise to "expectations," if not on her own part, on that of her family. Happy he, if he is not said to have been "trifling with her feelings," or "disappointing her hopes!" Under these circumstances, how can a man, who has any pride or any principle, become acquainted with a woman in such a manner as to *justify* them in marrying?

There are four ways in which people marry. First, accident or relationship has thrown them together in their childhood, and acquaintance has grown up naturally and unconsciously. Accordingly, in novels, it is generally cousins who marry; and *now* it seems the only natural thing—the only possible way of making an intimacy. And yet, we know that intermarriage between relations is in direct contravention of the laws of nature for the well-being of the race; witess the Quakers, the Spanish grandees, the royal races, the secluded valleys of mountainous countries, where madness, degeneration of race, defective organization and cretinism flourish and multiply.

The second way, and by far the most general, in which people marry, is this. A woman, thoroughly uninterested at home, and having formed a slight acquaintance with some accidental person, accepts him, if he "falls in love" with her, as it is technically called, and takes the chance. Hence the vulgar expression of marriage being a lottery, which it most truly is, for that the *right* two should come together has as many chances against it as there are blanks in any lottery.

The third way is, that some person is found sufficiently independent, sufficiently careless of the opinions of others, or sufficiently without modesty to speculate thus:—"It is worth while that I should become acquainted with so and so. I do not care what his or her opinion of me is, if, *after* having become acquainted, to do which can bear no other construction in people's eyes than a desire of marriage, I retreat." But there is this to be said, that it is doubtful whether, under this unnatural tension, which, to all susceptible characters, such a disregard of the opinions which they care for must be, a healthy or a natural feeling can grow up.

And now they are married—that is to say, two people have received the licence of a man in a white surplice. But they are no more man and wife for that than Louis XIV and the Infanta of Spain, married by proxy, were man and wife. The woman who has sold herself for an establishment, in what is she superior to those we may not name?

Lastly, in a few rare, very rare, cases, such as circumstances, always provided in novels, but seldom to be met with in real life, present—whether the accident of parents' neglect, or of parents' unusual skill and wisdom, or of having no parents at all, which is generally the case in novels—or marrying out of the person's rank of life, by which the usual restraints are removed, and there is room and play left for attraction—or extraordinary events, isolation, misfortunes, which many wish for, even though their imaginations be not tainted by romance-reading; such alternatives as these give food and space for the development of character and mutual sympathies.

But a girl, if she has any pride, is so ashamed of having any thing she wishes to say out of the hearing of her own family, she thinks it must be something so very wrong, that it is ten to one, if she have the opportunity of saying it, that she will not.

And yet she is spending her life, perhaps, in dreaming of accidental means of unrestrained communion.

And then it is thought pretty to say that "Women have no passion." If passion is excitement in the daily social intercourse with men, women think about marriage much more than men do; it is the only event of their lives. It ought to be a sacred event, but surely not the only event of a woman's life, as it is now. Many women spend their lives in asking men to marry them, in a refined way. Yet it is true that women are seldom in love. How can they be?

How cruel are the revulsions which high-minded women suffer! There was one who loved, in connexion with great deeds, noble thoughts, devoted feelings. They met after an interval. It was at one of those crowded parties of Civilization which we call Society. His only careless passing remark was, "The buzz to-night is like a manufactory." Yet he loved her.

V

"L'ENTHOUSIASME et la faiblesse d'un temps où l'intelligence monte très haut, entraînée par l'imagination, et tombe très bas, écrasée par une réalité, sans poésie et sans grandeur."

Women dream till they have no longer the strength to dream; those dreams against which they so struggle, so honestly, vigorously, and conscientiously, and so in vain, yet which are their life, without which they could not have lived; those dreams go at last. All their plans and visions seem vanished, and they know not where; gone and they cannot recall them. They do not even remember them. And they are left without the food either of reality or of hope.

Later in life, they neither desire nor dream, neither of activity, nor of love, nor of intellect. The last often survives the longest. They wish, if their experiences would benefit anybody, to give them to some one. But they never find an hour free in which to collect their thoughts, and so discouragement becomes ever deeper and deeper, and they less and less capable of undertaking anything.

It seems as if the female spirit of the world were mourning everlastingly over blessings, *not* lost, but which she has never had, and which, in her discouragement, she feels that she never will have, they are so far off.

The more complete a woman's organization, the more she will feel it, till at last there shall arise a woman, who will resume, in her own soul, all the sufferings of her race, and that woman will be the Saviour of her race.

Jesus Christ raised women above the condition of mere slaves, mere ministers to the passions of the man, raised them by this sympathy, to be ministers of God. He gave them moral activity. But the Age, the World, Humanity, must give them the means to exercise this moral activity, must give them intellectual cultivation, spheres of action.

There is perhaps no century where the woman shows so meanly as in this.* Because her education seems entirely to have parted company with her vocation; there is no longer unity between the woman as inwardly developed, and as outwardly manifested.

In the last century it was not so. In the succeeding one let us hope that it will no longer be so.

But now she is like the Archangel Michael as he stands upon Saint Angelo at Rome. She has an immense provision of wings, which seem as if they would bear her over earth and heaven; but when she tries to use them, she is petrified into stone, her feet are grown into the earth, chained to the bronze pedestal.

Nothing can well be imagined more painful than the present position of woman, unless, on the one hand, she renounces all outward activity and keeps herself within the magic sphere, the bubble of her dreams; or, on the other,

---

*At almost every period of social life, we find, as it were, two under currents running different ways. There is the noble woman who dreams the following out her useful vocation; but there is also the selfish dreamer now, who is ever turning to something new, regardless of the expectations she has voluntarily excited, who is ever talking about "making a life for herself," heedless that she is spoiling another life, undertaken, perhaps, at her own bidding. This is the ugly reverse of the medal.

surrendering all aspiration, she gives herself to her real life, soul and body. For those to whom it is possible, the latter is best; for out of activity may come thought, out of mere aspiration can come nothing.

But now—when the young imagination is so high and so developed, and reality is so narrow and conventional—there is no more parallelism between life in the thought and life in the actual than between the corpse, which lies motionless in its narrow bed, and the spirit, which, in our imagination, is at large among the stars.

The ideal life is passed in noble schemes of good consecutively followed up, of devotion to a great object, of sympathy given and received for high ideas and generous feelings. The actual life is passed in sympathy given and received for a dinner, a party, a piece of furniture, a house built or a garden laid out well, in devotion to your guests—(a too real devotion, for it implies that of all your time)—in schemes of schooling for the poor, which you follow up perhaps in an odd quarter of an hour, between luncheon and driving out in the carriage—broth and dripping are included in the plan—and the rest of your time goes in ordering the dinner, hunting for a governess for your children, and sending pheasants and apples to your poorer relations. Is there anything in *this* life which can be called an Incarnation of the ideal life within? Is it a wonder that the unhappy woman should prefer to keep them entirely separate? not to take the bloom off her Ideal by mixing it up with her Actual; not to make her Actual still more unpalatable by trying to *inform* it with her Ideal? And then she is blamed, and her own sex unites against her, for not being content with the "day of small things." She is told that "trifles make the sum of human things;" they do indeed. She is contemptuously asked, "Would she abolish domestic life?" Men are afraid that their houses will not be so comfortable, that their wives will make themselves "remarkable"—women, that they will make themselves distasteful to men; they write books (and very wisely) to teach themselves to dramatize "little things," to persuade themselves that "domestic life is their sphere" and to idealize the "sacred hearth." Sacred it is indeed. Sacred from the touch of their sons almost as soon as they are out of childhood—from its dulness and its tyrannous trifling *these* recoil. Sacred from the grasp of their daughters' affections, upon which it has so light a hold that they seize the first opportunity of marriage, *their* only chance of emancipation. The "sacred hearth;" sacred to their husband's sleep, their sons' absence in the body and their daughters' in mind.

Oh! mothers, who talk about this hearth, how much do you know of your sons' real life, how much of your daughters' imaginary one? Awake, ye women, all ye that sleep, awake! If this domestic life were so very good, would your young men wander away from it, your maidens think of something else?

The time is come when women must do something more than the "domestic hearth," which means nursing the infants, keeping a pretty house, having a good dinner and an entertaining party.

You say, "it is true, our young men see visions, and our maidens dream dreams, but what of? Does not the woman intend to marry, and have over again what she has at home? and the man ultimately too?" Yes, but not the same; she *will* have the same, that is, if circumstances are not altered to prevent it; but her *idéal* is very different, though that *idéal* and the reality will never come together to mould each other. And it is not only the unmarried woman who dreams. The married woman also holds long imaginary conversations but too often.

VI

WE LIVE IN THE WORLD, it is said, and must walk in its ways.

Was Christ called a complainer against the world? Yet all these great teachers and preachers must have had a most deep and ingrained sense, a continual gnawing feeling of the miseries and wrongs of the world. Otherwise they would not have been impelled to devote life and death to redress them. Christ, Socrates, Howard, they must have had no ear for the joys, compared to that which they had for the sorrows of the world.

They acted, however, and we complain. The great reformers of the world turn into the great misanthropists, if circumstances or organisation do not permit them to act. Christ, if He had been a woman, might have been nothing but a great complainer. Peace be with the misanthropists! They have made a step in progress; the next will make them great philanthropists; they are divided but by a line.

The next Christ will perhaps be a female Christ. But do we see one woman who looks like a female Christ? or even like "the messenger before" her "face," to go before her and prepare the hearts and minds for her?

To this will be answered that half the inmates of Bedlam begin in this way, by fancying that they are "the Christ."*

---

*It is quite true that insanity, sensuality, and monstrous fraud have constantly assumed to be "the Christ," *vide* the *Agapemone*, and the Mormons. "Believing" a man of the name of Prince "to be the tabernacle of God on earth," poor deluded women transfer to him all their stock in the Three per Cents. We hear of the Mormons, &c., being the "recipients and mouth-pieces of God's spirit." They profess to be "incarnations of the Deity," "witnesses of the Almighty, solely knowing God's will, and being the medium of communicating it to man," and so forth. It does not appear to us that this blasphemy is very dangerous to the cause of true religion in general, any more than forgery is very dangerous to commerce in general. It is the universal dishonesty in religion, as in trade, which is really dangerous.

People talk about imitating Christ, and imitate Him in the little trifling formal things, such as washing the feet, saying his prayer, and so on; but if any one attempts the real imitation of Him, there are no bounds to the outcry with which the presumption of that person is condemned.

For instance, Christ was saying something to the people one day, which interested Him very much, and interested them very much; and Mary and his brothers came in the middle of it, and wanted to interrupt Him, and take Him home to dinner, very likely — (how natural that story is! does it not speak more home than any historic evidences of the Gospel's reality?), and He, instead of being angry with their interruption of Him in such an important work for some trifling thing, answers, "Who is my mother? and who are my brethren? Whosoever shall do the will of my Father which is in heaven, the same is my brother and sister and mother." But if *we* were to say that, we should be accused of "destroying the family tie," of diminishing the obligation of the home duties.

He might well say, "Heaven and earth shall pass away, but my words shall not pass away." His words will never pass away. If He had said, "Tell them I am engaged at this moment in something very important; that the instruction of the multitude ought to go before any personal ties; that I will remember to come when I have done," no one would have been impressed by His words; but how striking is that, "Behold my mother and my brethren!"

VII

THE DYING WOMAN to her mourners: — "Oh! if you knew how gladly I leave this life, how much more courage I feel to take the chance of another, than of anything I see before me in this, you would put on your wedding-clothes instead of mourning for me!"

"But," they say, "so much talent! so many gifts! such good which you might have done!"

"The world will be put back some little time by my death," she says; "you see I estimate my powers at least as highly as you can; but it is by the death which has taken place some years ago in me, not by the death which is about to take place now." And so is the world put back by the death of every one who has to sacrifice the development of his or her peculiar gifts (which were meant, not for selfish gratification, but for the improvement of that world) to conventionality.

"My people were like children playing on the shore of the eighteenth century. I was their hobby-horse, their plaything; and they drove me to and fro, dear souls! never weary of the play themselves, till I, who had grown to woman's estate and to the ideas of the nineteenth century, lay down exhausted, my mind closed to hope, my heart to strength.

"Free — free — oh! divine freedom, art thou come at last? Welcome, beautiful death!"

Let neither name nor date be placed on her grave, still less the expression of regret or of admiration; but simply the words, "I believe in God."

Epilogue

"Florence Nightingale's Parts"
By Cynthia Macdonald

Were always straight, straight as her clothes:
The bow on her drawers, symmetrical as a butterfly;
The strings on her corselet like the pattern of a Morris
    Dance;
Her petticoats pleated like a fan, knife sharp;
The buttons on her dress lined in ranks;
The cameo brooch centered at the covered hollow of her
    neck;
And her part, straight through the waves as if
Moses commanded there. The whole divided as neatly
As the body divides itself by virtue of its pairs.

I, Florence Nightingale, take these wedded locks
To have and to hold, to pleat and to fold,
For richer for poorer, for better, for worse,
Lock, stock and barrel.
War makes more: more money, more disarray.
Take away the tray, Nellie, I shall eat nothing
This morning; I am fed up to the teeth.
O comb, my comb,
My honey, my hive, but only
The cocks can stride into battle.
I am at home without even a wattle.
For richer, for poorer, for better, for nurse.

Alone at home with *Mama* and *Papa*
And sister, Parthy, my sister,
Born in Greece like a fever blister.
Parthenope, Parthenope,
Watching my comb like a honey bee.
My comb inlaid with sea foam and mother of pearl,
Parting the waves like the prow of a ship.
A slip of a girl, a drowning, hair
Fanning out in the water
Like flame. Fame is no motive.
Right is. To set things right.
A knight enfolding the world in her black cloak,
Glints off her armor, the stars.
For richer, for poorer.

Crimea fever, Crimea fear.
To have and to hold.
The tableaux you planned, a guinea a head,
Will buy supplies sorely needed.
Assigning the princesses the parts
Of the graces should assure the subscription.
My thanks once again.
I am seen as austere. I am not.
Dreams of hair in tight curls,
Unplaited, unbound; first freedom
and lightness, then too light;
They are drawn into my mouth when I breathe.
I drown in my hair.
I am seen as austere. Death comes
From disorder. Partition the cabins.
Boil the sheets. Steer the course for home.
The mate throws the boatswain a Turkish bone.
A bonnet, blue as the vein of the Thames
On the map in the Captain's cabin where I work,
A bonnet will cover the loss of my hair when we land.
Crimea fever, a pox.

Cocks died, the hen did not.
I am spared for my work.
For richer, for poorer;
For better, for worse;
Till death us do part.

Florence Nightingale's parts were
Always straight. She saw to that using the mirror
On the desk which straddled her bed. Red velvet curtains
Hung like wattles from the posts
Between which she commanded:
Sanitation for India, Hospital Reorganization for
    Birmingham,
Tea for Disraeli.
Her hair grew back, pushing its rivulets
Against the will of her assignment,
But fell out again before she died at ninety,
Fell out completely. Baldness made no difference.
She parted her skin.

About Myra Stark

MYRA STARK has a Ph.D. in Victorian literature from New York University. She has published articles in numerous journals and is the co-editor of *In the Looking Glass: Twenty-One Modern Short Stories by Women.* She is currently co-editing two volumes on nineteenth-century English feminism in the Garland Reprint series. She lives with her husband and two children in New York City, where she teaches English literature and women's studies at Hunter College.

About Cynthia Macdonald

CYNTHIA MACDONALD lives in New York and has published two collections of poetry, "Amputations" and "Transplants," and a chapbook, "Pruning the Annuals." Her new collection, W(HOLES), will be published by Knopf in 1979. She currently heads a writing program in the English department at the University of Houston.

The **Feminist Press** promotes voices on the margins of dominant culture and publishes feminist works from around the world, inspiring personal transformation and social justice. We believe that books have the power to shift culture, and create a society free of violence, sexism, homophobia, racism, cis-supremacy, classism, sizeism, ableism and other forms of dehumanization. Our books and programs engage, educate, and entertain.

See our complete list of books at
feministpress.org

THE FEMINIST PRESS
AT THE CITY UNIVERSITY OF NEW YORK
FEMINISTPRESS.ORG